# *Be Beautiful Mentally*:
## Who Told You You Weren't Beautiful?

*Keedra A. Keeley*

Front and Back Cover Illustration by 225 Designs

First Edition

Copyright © 2015 by Keedra A. Keeley

ISBN-13: 978-0692580431 (Be Beautiful)
ISBN-10: 0692580433

Published By: Keedra A. Keeley and I Will Be Beautiful, Inc.
Atlanta, GA

Printed in the United States of America

All rights reserved. No part of this book may be reproduced, stored in retrieval systems, or transmitted in any form, by any means, including mechanical, electronic, photocopying, recording or otherwise, without prior written permission of the publisher.

## ~ACKNOWLEDGEMENTS~

I would not be the person that I am if it weren't for my parents, Rev. Andre E. Keeley, Sr. and Mrs. Robyn Walker. For all the good they have done in my life, and even for all the not so good they have done in my life. All of it has created me to be the woman that I am. I am eternal grateful for your never ending support in everything that I do. Even when you don't have it, you make sure I do, and I appreciate that beyond words that I can use to describe.

My family has always been my support system. My brother, my grandparents, my aunts, uncles, and cousins. I really could not do anything if I did not know they were going to always be there to be my foundation.

Rev. Carolyn A. L. McCrary, Th.D., Jarena Lee Professor of Pastoral Theology, Care and Counseling Coordinator, and Doctor of Theology Program In Pastoral Counseling, and Dr. Itihari Toure Ed.D, faculty for Religious Education, both professors at the Interdenominational Theological Center in Atlanta, GA, who have deposited more in my life than they know. Dr. Toure you are the epitome of wisdom, Proverbs 8 personified. Your creativity and the small sips of wisdom I have been able to draw from your wisdom well during my short time at the ITC contributes immensely to my life, my ministry, and it never fails to touch my spirit. Dr. McCrary, I cannot even sum up in words to describe your contribution to my being, my journey, and my ministry. Thank you for being everything I needed when I needed it, even

when you don't even realize it. The lens in which I look through to see my path has been dusted off simply by the two of you.

My very best friends Monet, Andrea, and Erica. Thank you for being the constants in my life and allowing me to know what healthy, loving, and supportive relationships between real women look like and feel like. Thank you for never wavering in your friendship and for loving me just the way I am.

JJ, I wouldn't have been able to do Seminary without you and your friendship! I am forever grateful to be able to call you my best friend!!

My Pastor, Rev. Christopher M. Waller and my Dean, Dr. Paul L. Brown. Thank you for holding me down in the ways that you have through my educational process. Words cannot describe my appreciation for your support and your belief in me through your support.

Everyone who has ever supported me in whatever endeavor I decide to embark upon, I appreciate each and every one of you. My journey would not be one to take if I did not have the support of all of the people who surround me.

For all of you, I am forever and eternally Grateful!

## ~DEDICATION~

I know books are usually dedicated to someone other than yourself, but being this is my first book, I want to dedicate this book to myself. Not everyone has a vision, turns it into a dream, and goes after that dream to make it a reality. To you Keedra from me Keedra: I dedicate your first book to you. Thank you for not giving up, thank you for trusting in God, thank you for not letting anyone stop you or deter you, thank you for being the ambitious, determined, honest, woman with a genuine good heart. Thank you for staying true to yourself, thank you for learning from your mistakes, thank you for enduring the heartaches, the tears, the disappointments long enough to be able to write about them. Thank you for becoming aware of who, what, and why you are. Thank you for teaching yourself that you are Beautiful, thank you for holding on to those teachings. Thank you for seeking knowledge, truth and wisdom no matter how hard the path gets. Thank you for your relationship with God. Rest assured your husband will be God's heart in human flesh. Thank you for caring about someone besides yourself enough to allow yourself to be vulnerable enough to be a healing agent. Thank you. To you, with love, I dedicate this book!

## ~FROM THE AUTHOR ~

*Be Beautiful Mentally: Who Told You You Weren't Beautiful?* starts by taking a look at those things we do not like about ourselves, and finding beauty in them; whether it is changing how we look at them or changing them all together. This book will take you through a month's journey of how to change negative thoughts about yourself into positive thoughts about yourself, creating positive energy within your own personal sacred space. I do not guarantee that your negative thoughts will fully be positive ones by the end of the month, but I do guarantee that you will have a better understanding as to **<u>how</u>** to change the way you feel about yourself as it pertains to the things you do not like about yourself. I am not a licensed therapist, I do not claim to have all of the answers, but I do stand firm on what has worked for me in my process of becoming Beautiful Mentally for myself. And to be quite honest with you, I still have to go through the process every day. One thing I can say, as you go along and continue to do the work on yourself, it does get easier. Where it used to take me months to just achieve one piece of understanding about myself, I am now able to reach a place of understanding much quicker.

I have shared a piece of my sacred and intimate space with you through this book. As the late and great poet Langston Hughes said, "Life ain't been no crystal stair", and it has been quite a journey trying to make it and keep going up those stairs. But I have faith in God. And just in case there is someone else out there who has not lived a rose colored life and wear the

scars on the inside every day, my desire is to offer hope to other women who want to give up, who need an extra push, or needs to be reminded that they are *B*eautiful.

All of the *Be* *B*eautiful Books are designed to help you become self-aware in all of the target areas: Mentally, Emotionally, Spiritually, Physically, and Personally. As you go through each book, the process that you are learning should become easier and heighten your level of self-awareness. This is an on-going process that should not stop after each book. Each book is designed to help you incorporate each practice into your daily life whenever applicable.

It is best to start this book on a day that you don't have to work, don't have to run the kids all over town, or don't have too many obligations to anyone else. This is a journey for you, so I suggest the first day you start this process, you are able to dedicate time for yourself to read the beginning of the first week, reflect, and to begin the work. It is my prayer, that by the time you reach the end of this book, you have been equipped with the tools to continue the journey of making a positive change about the way you think about yourself on your own.

Be Blessed, *Be* *B*eautiful!

*Keedra* ☺

## ~CONTENTS~

## SECTION ONE

| | |
|---|---|
| Who Told You? A Historical Account of Beauty Defined | 1 |
| Defining Beauty | 8 |
| Defining Mental Strength | 11 |

## SECTION TWO

| | |
|---|---|
| Week 1: Identifying Those Things I Don't Like About Myself | 15 |
| Week 2: Changing Those Things I Don't Like About Myself | 37 |
| Week 3: Naming Those Things I Am Good At Doing | 59 |
| Week 4: Visualizing And Manifesting The Person I Want To Be | 75 |

## SECTION THREE

| | |
|---|---|
| Appendix | 99 |

# SECTION ONE

## WHO TOLD YOU?: A HISTORICAL ACCOUNT OF BEAUTY DEFINED

Throughout history, women have carried many burdens and have endured many struggles. Women have carried their burdens and endured their struggles both as individuals through their own personal experiences, and collectively as a community of women. Ultimately those burdens and struggles turn into a source of added hurt and pain, running so deep they become consuming. So much so, women find themselves operating out of hurt and pain, and their focus is shifted to coping with the pain rather than healing the pain. For some, they know what their personal burdens and struggles are, the cause of them, and they actively work to bring their selves to a healthy place. For others, they go through life's journey without knowing what it is that truly pains them, and unable to recognize the results of their pain in order to correct it. Healing hurt and pain requires going to the root, but that is a difficult thing to do when you don't understand where the root begins. The result, an embedded self-hate constructed by someone or something other than yourself.

In his book *The Conspiracy to Destroy Black Women*, author Michael Porter writes "The worst form of female crucifixion is self-hate. Every woman in America is a victim of a White male supremacist, self-hate, instilling socialization. From the cradles to the grave, American and many other Western women are taught to be displeased with their weight or skin color or hair texture or hair length or breast size or eye color or nose and lip size."[1] It seems as though it is easier to teach one how to first hate their physical appearance, planting the practice of self-hate to take its root. It then moves into other areas of a woman's life, ultimately transforming her mind to not only hate her physical appearance, but then finding other reasons to hate other aspects of who she is, what she is, and why she is. Or even creating a correlation between a negative perception she may carry of herself, her feeling of lack of intelligence for example, and her physical appearance, thinking that one is a direct influence of the other. Leaving her to ask the questions such as "Am I unintelligent because I am unattractive?"

At the same token, as women are taught how to self-hate, not as often enough are they taught how to self-love by understanding, accepting, loving and embracing their own selves and each other. We are shown on all types of media outlets, one of society's biggest influencers, women fighting each other and damaging each other's name for the uplift of their own. So the self-hate metamorphoses into hurt and pain, hurt and pain transmutes into the struggles and the burdens we carry, and we eventually end up being self-inflictors of our own struggles and burdens because we fail to identify the root of our own self-hate.

In her book *Womanism Against Socially-Constructed Matriarchal Images: A Theoretical Model Toward A Therapeutic Goal*, author Markeva Gwendolyn Hill believes "The construction of the African American female's social and emotional location, the manner in which she perceives herself, and the manner in which she is perceived by today's society, evolved from the

African diaspora and slavery."[2] If we look back in American History, to the enslaved African woman and the White American slave owner's wife, we see two different women, yet both are subjugated to oppression. Oppressed by what someone else told them about who they were. Someone told that enslaved African woman that she was less than human and considered property, that she was not worth anything, that she was too black, that she was not smart, that she had no value or worth, and that she was nothing more than Massa's sexual release as she was violated as a woman. Someone told the White American slave owner's wife that while she was better than the enslaved African woman she was less than equal to her husband, the White American male, and even sometimes considered to be his property as well. Someone told her that while she was better than the enslaved African woman, she still had no rights as a woman. Someone told the White American slave owner's wife that while she was better than the enslaved African woman, the degradation, abuse, rape, and exploitation of another woman was ok. I know there are more ethnicities that make up America today, but my point is that no matter the race, no matter the ethnicity, no matter the country of origin, oppression is not a respecter of any of them.

Michael Porter addresses the issue of self-hate among African American women and boldly identifies the root. "African American women were victims of White male supremacist instilled self-hate long before the 1920's. The African woman's body was used as a public restroom by White men. She was

simultaneously despised, lusted after, and raped by White men. Although her Black skin and full figure were historical symbols of *B*eauty, she was placed in the non-human category by racist power holders who, nonetheless, desired her and used her for sexual entertainment. What one must realize is that the African American woman began in the holes of Western slave ships."[3]

On the flipside, the patriarchal White male power structure has even defined what *B*eauty is for White women as well, which is based on the profit they can gain from it. Where they were once told their thin lips were a standard of *B*eauty, they are now looking to fill and plump them up. Where they were once told a small frame was a standard of *B*eauty, they are now seeking synthetic enhancements to their bodies to mirror the voluptuousness of the Black and Latino woman.

For many centuries, the white male power structure has impaired non-White women by making the White woman the standard for *B*eauty. Light skin became more *B*eautiful than darker skin. Straight hair became more *B*eautiful than naturally kinky curly hair. Light eyes became more *B*eautiful than darker eyes. A thin shaped figure became more *B*eautiful than a full figured woman. The list runs long of those negative influences that oppress us and tell us who we are not, who we are supposed to be, what we are not, what we are supposed to be, why we are not, and why we are supposed to be when it comes to *B*eauty. When we believe those influences we have become

oppressed, and oppression causes hurt and it causes pain. Unfortunately, having always been told as women who we are, what we are and why we are, this has been passed down through generations, each affecting the next in various, more traumatic, ways. We find ourselves, as women, mentally stuck and unable to break free from the different psychological chains we all wear.

This vicious cycle must be broken because it is stripping us of who we really are as women and out of our rightful positions in this world, as women. We have lost respect for ourselves both individually and as a community. We have lost respect for each other, both individually and as a community. We are struggling to find a sense of value and worth for ourselves both individually and as a community. We are listening to the voices and watching the images that try to define us as women both individually and as a community. We have to free ourselves of these things that we have been told about who, what and why we are, both individually, and as a community.

Women have to begin asking themselves "who told you?" as the first step to healing the embedded psychological trauma that has been imposed upon them. Who told you all of the things that you think about yourself? Who shaped your perception of yourself? The answers to these questions are limitless, but once we focus in on finding the root to our hurt and pain, we can then begin to experience truly healing, both individually and as a community.

In his book *Breaking the Chains of Psychological Slavery*, author Na'im Akbar identifies that "the primary objective to freeing the [Black] mind is to change the consciousness."[4] He continues to suggest that changing the mind requires us to change the information that is fed to the mind. Although in his book Akbar is primarily discussing how today's Black community can free themselves from the mental oppression that has been embedded in them since slavery, his message is to a mentally oppressed marginalized people. Women too can fall under this category of the marginalized mentally oppressed.

Akbar says that "'knowledge of self' which was the foundation of the highly successful [Black] reform program of the Honorable Elijah Muhammad (1965) and the premise of Ancient African teachers in the Nile Valley over 4,000 years ago, still remains an essential ingredient of this process of mental liberation. A fundamental component of the chains which continue to handicap [Black] minds is the excessive and distorted information...and the absence of information about ourselves."[5]

The key to changing the way we think about our own selves as women lies in the knowledge that we seek for ourselves about ourselves. When we actively work to get to know who we are, what we are, and why we are, we begin to break the chains of embeddedness that have been passed down. We disrupt the plans of those who only seek to gain and profit from our lack of self-knowledge. We empower not only ourselves but we empower other women to be whole and complete based on who the say they are. When we actively seek

knowledge about our own selves we change our mentality and ultimately changing our future and our children's future. When we seek knowledge about who we are, what we are, and why we are we begin to define *Beauty* based on our own terms and standards, instead of those whose agenda is to keep us oppressed. Know thyself, to empower thyself, to free thyself, to allow thyself to *Be Beautiful!*

## ~DEFINING BEAUTY~

If I asked you to write down words that described beauty, what would you write? How would you define or describe beauty? Then I would ask who informed you that these descriptions and definitions represented beauty? Western society has given us a standard of beauty: small waist, long hair, straight hair, for skin tones that contain melanin the lighter the skin the more beautiful, white skin tones, full eyelashes, and light colored eyes. Unfortunately, women draw their self-esteem from these standards of beauty that are fed to us.

But there are many forms of Beauty as it pertains to a woman. Mentally, Emotionally, Spiritually, Physically, and Personally are, to me, all the components that make a woman whole and complete. It is in these five components that I have come to define true beauty.

To *Be Beautiful* Mentally is a mentality. It is to be mentally strong and stable, to be a positive thinker, and to have healthy thoughts toward one's own self. Our thoughts are very powerful and they have the ability to dictate everything about ourselves and our lives. If the Bible is your choice of spiritual inspiration and empowerment, Philippians 4:8 gives a guide as to how we should conduct our thoughts and that is on good things. When we fail to have a strong, powerful, and healthy mentality we fail to honor who, what, and why we are as women.

To 𝓑e 𝓑eautiful Emotionally is to be emotionally stable. As women, we tend to be very emotional. It is ok to have emotions, it is a good thing and a sign that you are human. It is when we let our emotions cloud our judgement and cause us to act irrational that our emotions are not healthy. When we act on impulse based on our emotional state instead of experiencing our emotions, riding out the emotional wave, and *then* deciding on a course of action, we fail to honor who, what, and why we are as women.

To 𝓑e 𝓑eautiful Spiritually is to be connected to your inner spirit. This is obtained through prayer, meditation, and personal reflection. Being and staying connected to the spiritual power that works inside of you is essential for obtaining success in all other 𝓑e 𝓑eautiful target areas. It creates balance, tranquility, peace, and understanding, that's why it falls in the middle of all the target areas. When we are lost and can't find a sense of peace within ourselves, is when our spiritual nature needs to be nurtured. As women, our roles and contributions to human existence are vital, so it is important that we are first plugged in to spirit. When we fail to actively and consistently nurture our spirit, we fail to honor who, what, and why we are as women.

To 𝓑e 𝓑eautiful Physically is to love and appreciate the natural skin you are in, and living a healthy lifestyle. This includes Black women loving their skin tones and complexions whether it is light skin, brown skin, dark skin, or mixed skin. It includes embracing your natural hair texture. It includes embracing your natural physical features. It includes embracing a healthy lifestyle in order to take care of your temple. It includes knowing your Beauty is not defined by your body type and size, but keeping healthiness as an obtainable goal. It is understanding what a woman's body is created for, and using it responsibly. When we fail to embrace our physical selves just the way we are then we fail to honor who, what, and why we are as women.

To Be Beautiful Personally is to know who you are, what you are, and why you are. As women, we play many different roles, to many different people, at many different times. So making sure to take the time out for yourself for self-care, to connect with yourself, and to love on yourself allows you to learn how to love yourself first. Loving on yourself is essential to Being Beautiful because just as the saying goes, if you don't love you, how you can you expect anyone else to love you, or how you can expect to know how to love anyone else. When we fail to explore who we really are and learn to love on ourselves, then we fail to honor who, what, and why we are as women.

Be Beautiful! It's Your Right!

## ~ DEFINING MENTAL STRENGTH ~

**What does it mean to be mentally strong?**

According to the dictionary, the word strong means to be powerful, to have authority, to be firm, and of great courage. If we apply this definition to the way we think, then to be mentally strong means to think with power and authority, to be firm in what we think, and to be courageous in how we think. It's easy to give in to certain thoughts, especially if they are negative, which ultimately influence our behaviors.

**Why is it important to be mentally strong?**

It is important to be mentally strong because when you are, it is not easy for your thoughts and your mind to be easily influenced in a negative way. That is not to be confused with not being able to have an opened mind and welcoming new thoughts, but it does mean you stand firm on your beliefs before falling for just anything that anyone is trying to serve you.

**How does being mentally strong make me a better woman?**

When you are a mentally strong woman, you have made up in your mind the positives about who you are, what you are, and why you are. Another way to look at it, you have also made up in your mind the negatives about who you are not, what you are not, and why you are not. This makes you a better person and woman because no matter how someone else may try to categorize you, may try to define you, may try to influence you,

may try to tell you about who and what you are as a woman, you have already determined all of those things for yourself and the likelihood of thinking and conforming to something otherwise is not as great as if you were not mentally strong.

There are many components that make up being mentally strong. Some of these components include how you view and think about yourself, how you control yourself, how you view and think about your situations, how you handle your situations, how you view and think about others, how you handle others, and your core beliefs and values. It is my belief that if you can master the art of first having a strong mentality, then achieving Beauty in all of the other Be Beautiful target areas – emotionally, spiritually, physically, and personally – will be easier for you.

Being mentally strong is being mentally healthy. When you think positively it affects the energy within you and around you, and you produce positive results. You may not always think positive about yourself on everything, you may not always look at every situation through a positive lens, and you may not think positively toward everyone. So it is my hope that Be Beautiful Mentally can teach you how to process those thoughts so that you can begin to turn all of your negative thoughts into healthy, positive, productive ones.

# SECTION TWO

## WEEK ONE

## Identifying Those Things I Don't Like About Myself

*"when there is no enemy within, the enemies outside cannot hurt you"*

—african proverb

The very first lesson I had to learn when it came to the way I think about myself is that someone else cannot tell me something about myself that I already know. If it was something negative about me, someone could not tell me anything negative about myself in an attempt to control me or my thinking. If it was something positive about myself, I thanked them for the compliment, but because I already knew it for myself I did not depend on their compliment to validate me or to boost my self-esteem.

I first became aware of some of the things I did not like about myself back in high school. Although looking back now, I don't agree with some of the things I did not like about myself and the reasons for which I did not like them, but the fact is I started paying attention to myself. The journey from there has not been the easiest, but it has been the most rewarding and the most fulfilling. Those things I did not like about myself were based on the things I liked about other people, or I thought I liked about other people. I remember thinking how I was quiet among my group of friends. There were some who were more talkative and at a much larger volume than I, and they always seemed to keep all of us laughing and entertained. This was unconsciously informing me that in order to have the attention of others like they do, I must act like they do. So I remember telling myself to try and be more talkative and a little louder. Looking back, what I did not realize then that I do now was that I did not need to draw attention to myself in that way because truth be told that's all I was really seeking. And now I find that I do appreciate and I do embrace the quiet side of me.

    Since high school, it took me a great amount of time to become fully aware of myself. Through the years, simply by paying attention to who I was, I learned what I liked and what I did not like. I learned why I reacted in certain ways to certain things and noticed how I chose to react. I learned what made me very happy and those things that made me very sad. I learned how and why I interacted with certain people in certain ways. I learned what motivated me and what made me depressed. I learned how I liked to be treated by other people and how I did not like being treated. I learned my strengths and my weaknesses. I learned what I wanted to spend my life doing and discovering how I was going to accomplish those things. Basically, through the years, I learned me! I learned me in and out, backwards and forwards, forwards and backward.

    In the process of learning me, I began to take notice to what was healthy and unhealthy about the reasons behind not liking some things about myself. I had to find my way to the root of the dislike so I could determine how I wanted to change it. What I soon learned was that there were so many reasons that could contribute to the root of my dislikes, but it was ultimately how I was being informed and what I was being informed about. The reality check that I experienced was that I had to be honest with myself about those reasons in order to fully evaluate and determine whether or not the things I did not like about myself were for healthy or unhealthy reasons. It is not easy being honest with yourself about yourself. We all want to feel good about ourselves and see ourselves in a positive light. We sometimes dance around our issues and make excuses for them.

Or I have even totally ignored them all together because that just was not what I wanted to admit for myself. Eventually what I found was that honesty was therapeutic and it was healing, no matter how brutal the truth was. I would have to say those were probably the toughest parts of my growing process but also the very pivotal points as well. This was when true growth began to take place and I was able to really do the work on myself.

Defining what is healthy and what is unhealthy is not always easy and can sometimes be a thin line. To determine whether the traits I did not like about myself were healthy and unhealthy, I asked myself "how does this make me a better person?" For instance, if I disliked that I had a nasty attitude toward people which ended up making them feel bad, this does not make me a better person. Therefore, this thing that I dislike about myself is unhealthy and needs to be changed to something healthy. If I dislike about myself the fact that I am too nice and too giving because I always feel taken advantage of at the end, when determining whether or not this is something healthy or unhealthy, I ask if this makes me a better person. And in fact, it does. So, it is something about me that is actually healthy, and I have to now learn when to be nice and giving, and how to be nice and giving without feeling like I was taken advantage of. What I eventually arrived at was an appreciation for myself and realizing how rare it is these days for someone to just be nice and giving without expecting anything in return. So the thing that I once disliked about myself, I now embrace and appreciate more than anything because I know that it is something rare to find, and I am able to be nice and giving without looking for anything back in return. It makes me love me even more because now I see not only my quality, but myself, as a person who is rare that you do not come across every day.

As I mentioned, there are many reasons that contribute to the root of your dislikes. And no one knows the answer and can find the answer but you. In my opinion all things are ultimately due to a lack of self-love and a lack of self-confidence. The reasons behind either one of those can be varying. One of my root issues was that I did not like being alone, and what I ultimately realized was that the reasons that contributed to me not liking to be alone was because I did not love myself, did not know how to love myself, and I wanted someone else to do it for me. We can all agree that it feels so good when someone else loves on us. But what we fail to realize is that the one thing that stays constant in our lives, next to God, is our own selves. What happens when the love we depend on from someone else is no longer there? Well, nine times out of ten, we go looking for it in other places. And because we are so desperate for it, we will settle for what *appears* to us to be love. We create this vicious cycle and we fall further and further away from truly loving ourselves.

Everyone wants to give and wants to receive love. As my good friend, author D. Westfield of *The Audacity to Love* book series would say, "Love is the apex of life." The reasons behind why we do what we do are because of love. We have this innate desire within us to always be in a constant exchange of love by

either giving or receiving it. And most of the time we aspire to receive it more than we aspire to give it.

The person we must learn to love first and foremost is ourselves. That includes accepting those things we dislike about ourselves and finding the strength to do the necessary work to get to the core of it and make the appropriate changes. No one is going to teach you how to love yourself better than you. It is through this exchange within yourself you learn to truly love others. Yes, it is an exchange within yourself. You have to learn how to give your own self love, and you have to learn how to receive and accept love from your own self as well.

### WHO TOLD YOU?

As I think long, hard and deep, I would have to say that when it came to not loving myself, it was myself who informed my own self that I was not good enough. There were traits that I admired about other people that I felt I did not possess. So I tried to be like them instead of recognizing who I was and the traits that I already possessed. I failed to understand that being different was a good thing. I failed to learn who and what I was so I could appreciate who and what I was.

### RECAP:

- You have to be completely honest with yourself about the things you dislike about yourself and the reasons why you dislike them

- Honesty is therapeutic and healing, no matter how brutal the truth is
- Ask yourself questions, such as how and why, to learn about yourself and uncover your hidden truths
- When determining whether the things you dislike about yourself are healthy or unhealthy, ask yourself the question "How does this make me a better person?"
- The person we must learn to love first and foremost is our self

## LET'S DO THE WORK!

Directions: Each day you will evaluate yourself and identify something you do not like about yourself. Those dislikes can include both physical features and character/personality traits. Try to get a good and fair number of each so you address you as a whole person and not just from one aspect. Don't worry, we will have an entire book dedicated to physical features in *Be Beautiful Physically*. Once you have identified something you dislike about yourself, follow the instructions to really work through your dislike and get to the root of where it came from. In other words, figuring out Who Told You? You will have a morning exercise, and an evening exercise. Track your daily progress in your *Be Beautiful* Journal component by going through your day, recording your actions, your emotions, your thoughts, your challenges, and how you managed the overall process.

Understanding each questions:

**1. One thing I do not like about myself is.......?**

Identify something about yourself that makes you think negatively about yourself. This could be something physical, a certain attitude you have, a certain emotion that you experience.....anything that is a part of who you are, what you do, how you act, and/or how you think.

**2. The first time I learned this was negative was...**
Identify the first time you learned that what you dislike about your self was something negative. Was it by watching something on TV, seeing something on social media, during a family function, in the middle of an argument, hanging with friends and so forth? Identify the circumstances around the situation that led you to begin believing this was negative.

**3. The first person who I heard say this was something negative was...**
Identify who the key person was, or key persons were, in leading you to believe this was something negative. Was it a public figure, a friend, a family member, girlfriend/boyfriend, husband/wife, etc.?

**4. I listened to them because...**
What was it about that person that allowed you to believe this was something negative? Find within yourself your own answers, but some examples can include because they were someone who you trusted, someone who you admired, someone who you loved, etc.

**5. I listened to them because I...**
What was it about you that allowed you to believe this was something negative? Find within yourself your own answers, but some examples can include because I did not have a positive example, because I was easily influenced, because I trusted the person who said it, etc.

**6. Identify a feeling from the Feelings Inventory Wheel in the Appendix that is associated with this negative perception.**
When you think about this thing, do you feel sad, mad, angry, hurt, etc.

**7. Is this something that could actually be seen as healthy or unhealthy? Why or why not?**

Sometimes when we change the way we view something it changes whether or not we can consider it something healthy or unhealthy. Could you possibly change the way you view the things you don't like about yourself in order to see it as something healthy?

**Day 1:**
*Morning:*

One thing I do not like about myself is _____

_____

  Throughout the course of the day think about the possible root of this dislike. Ask yourself questions such as "Am I comparing myself to someone else?", or "What is it about this quality or trait that makes me wish I did not possess it?", or "How does this quality or trait make me treat myself and/or others?" Dig deep into why you chose this as something that you don't like about yourself. And remember to be honest.

  Until you are really in tune and aware of your feelings, to REALLY get to the root of this one thing can actually take some time, much longer than a week even. But this will teach you how to get to a point where you recognize those things and are able to make the first steps to evaluating them and correcting them however necessary.

*Evening:*

The first time I learned this was negative was _____

_____

_____

The first person who I heard say this was a negative thing was

_____

_____

I listened to them because they were _____

_____

I listened to them because I _____

_____

Identify a feeling or feelings from the Feelings Inventory Wheel in the Appendix that is associated with this negative perception.

_____

Is this something that could actually be seen as healthy or unhealthy?  Why or why not? _____

_____

**Day 2:**

*Morning:*

One thing I do not like about myself is _____

_____

     Throughout the course of the day think about the possible root of this dislike. Ask yourself questions such as "Am I comparing myself to someone else?", or "What is it about this quality or trait that makes me wish I did not possess it?", or "How does this quality or trait make me treat myself and/or others?" Dig deep into why you chose this as something that you don't like about yourself. And remember to be honest.

     Until you are really in tune and aware of your feelings, to REALLY get to the root of this one thing can actually take some time, much longer than a week even. But this will teach you how to get to a point where you recognize those things and are able to make the first steps to evaluating them and correcting them however necessary.

*Evening:*

The first time I learned this was negative was _____

_____

_____

The first person who I heard say this was a negative thing was

_____

_____

I listened to them because they were _____

_____

I listened to them because I _____

_____

Identify a feeling or feelings from the Feelings Inventory Wheel in the Appendix that is associated with this negative perception.

_____

Is this something that could actually be seen as healthy or unhealthy? Why or why not? _____

_____

**Day 3:**

*Morning:*

One thing I do not like about myself is _____

_____

      Throughout the course of the day think about the possible root of this dislike. Ask yourself questions such as "Am I comparing myself to someone else?", or "What is it about this quality or trait that makes me wish I did not possess it?", or "How does this quality or trait make me treat myself and/or others?" Dig deep into why you chose this as something that you don't like about yourself. And remember to be honest.

      Until you are really in tune and aware of your feelings, to REALLY get to the root of this one thing can actually take some time, much longer than a week even. But this will teach you how to get to a point where you recognize those things and are able to make the first steps to evaluating them and correcting them however necessary.

*Evening:*

The first time I learned this was negative was _____

_____

_____

The first person who I heard say this was a negative thing was

_____

_____

I listened to them because they were _____

_____

I listened to them because I _____

_____

Identify a feeling or feelings from the Feelings Inventory Wheel in the Appendix that is associated with this negative perception.

_____

Is this something that could actually be seen as healthy or unhealthy? Why or why not? _____

_____

**Day 4:**

*Morning:*

One thing I do not like about myself is _____

_____

    *Throughout the course of the day think about the possible root of this dislike. Ask yourself questions such as "Am I comparing myself to someone else?", or "What is it about this quality or trait that makes me wish I did not possess it?", or "How does this quality or trait make me treat myself and/or others?" Dig deep into why you chose this as something that you don't like about yourself. And remember to be honest.*

    *Until you are really in tune and aware of your feelings, to REALLY get to the root of this one thing can actually take some time, much longer than a week even. But this will teach you how to get to a point where you recognize those things and are able to make the first steps to evaluating them and correcting them however necessary.*

*Evening:*

The first time I learned this was negative was _____

_____

_____

The first person who I heard say this was a negative thing was

_____

_____

I listened to them because they were _____

_____

I listened to them because I _____

_____

Identify a feeling or feelings from the Feelings Inventory Wheel in the Appendix that is associated with this negative perception.

_____

Is this something that could actually be seen as healthy or unhealthy? Why or why not? _____

_____

## Day 5:

*Morning:*

One thing I do not like about myself is _____

_____

     *Throughout the course of the day think about the possible root of this dislike. Ask yourself questions such as "Am I comparing myself to someone else?", or "What is it about this quality or trait that makes me wish I did not possess it?", or "How does this quality or trait make me treat myself and/or others?" Dig deep into why you chose this as something that you don't like about yourself. And remember to be honest.*

     *Until you are really in tune and aware of your feelings, to REALLY get to the root of this one thing can actually take some time, much longer than a week even. But this will teach you how to get to a point where you recognize those things and are able to make the first steps to evaluating them and correcting them however necessary.*

*Evening:*

The first time I learned this was negative was _____

_____

_____

The first person who I heard say this was a negative thing was

_____

_____

I listened to them because they were _____

_____

I listened to them because I _____

_____

Identify a feeling or feelings from the Feelings Inventory Wheel in the Appendix that is associated with this negative perception.

_____

Is this something that could actually be seen as healthy or unhealthy? Why or why not? _____

_____

**Day 6:**

*Morning:*

One thing I do not like about myself is _____

_____

    *Throughout the course of the day think about the possible root of this dislike. Ask yourself questions such as "Am I comparing myself to someone else?", or "What is it about this quality or trait that makes me wish I did not possess it?", or "How does this quality or trait make me treat myself and/or others?" Dig deep into why you chose this as something that you don't like about yourself. And remember to be honest.*

    *Until you are really in tune and aware of your feelings, to REALLY get to the root of this one thing can actually take some time, much longer than a week even. But this will teach you how to get to a point where you recognize those things and are able to make the first steps to evaluating them and correcting them however necessary.*

*Evening:*

The first time I learned this was negative was _____

_____

_____

The first person who I heard say this was a negative thing was

_____

_____

I listened to them because they were _____

_____

I listened to them because I _____

_____

Identify a feeling or feelings from the Feelings Inventory Wheel in the Appendix that is associated with this negative perception.

_____

Is this something that could actually be seen as healthy or unhealthy?  Why or why not? _____

_____

## CONSECRATION

      The word consecrate means to make or declare sacred. This week you have done what can be considered hard work on yourself as you dug deep into some things that you have probably been holding on to for quite some time, and have been

causing you hurt and pain. So the work that you did this week to uncover truths about yourself can be declared sacred.

As a symbol of this sacred declaration, find a rock and a large bowl of water. As you hold the rock in your hand, recall to memory all of the things you identified this week that you did not like about yourself. Let the rock be a symbol of all of these negative things that have been holding you down. Now drop the rock in the bowl of water. Let the water symbolize a purifying agent, as it purifies you of all of the negative things that have been holding you down. Declare to yourself, that from this day forth, you will no longer allow these negative thoughts about yourself take up any space in your mind. Take the bowl of water and dump it outside into grass or soil. This allows the universe to now work in conjunction with you on your behalf.

~~~~~

Congratulations!! You have successfully completed Week 1 of your own *Be Beautiful* Challenge! I know this week had the possibility to be mentally draining, but the hard part is over! You were honest with yourself, you thought things through, and you provided yourself with some very helpful and thought provoking answers. You should be very proud of yourself for your hard work! Take the next day, Day 7, off to mentally and emotionally relax, and prepare yourself for Week 2. Go take a look in the mirror. I see the *Beauty* beginning to shine through already, don't you?

## WEEK TWO

## Changing Those Things I Don't Like About Myself

*"life is not about finding yourself, it's about creating yourself"*

—george bernard shaw

Last week we focused on identifying those things that we dislike about ourselves and getting to the root of why we have these dislikes. We took a look at the initial root of each dislike and how those dislikes really make us feel when we face them. We also thought through whether or not this dislike was something unhealthy or something healthy but we just did not realize it. Some of you may be taking a real hard look at yourself and feeling like these dislikes play a huge role in the person that you are. Some of you may be feeling low in self-esteem from identifying your dislikes about yourself. Some of you may be excited about finally learning how to understand yourself more. I have experienced all of these emotions before so I am going to say that these feelings are natural and normal. I went from not liking myself more than what I already did to embracing my weaknesses and turning them into my strengths.

This week we are going to work on turning our dislikes into likes. There was a time that I used to always get my heart broken. I hated about myself that I was so open to love and often times wished I was as hard as a rock. So often I tried to be cold hearted and not have any emotions, but I only found myself fighting against myself. I disliked the fact that I had emotions, real emotions, and they were not afraid to show themselves for any occasion, be it happy or sad. This made me feel too vulnerable, too weak. I remember feeling like something really was wrong with me, and I hated that I did not know how to change it. I cried long, hard and often over it.

I spent years fighting against myself, trying to train my mind and my heart to not care and to not put so much energy

into what I was feeling when I felt it. I found myself putting forth so much energy that I became exhausted mentally, emotionally, spiritually, and physically, and that exhaustion eventually led to one of many depressing periods in my life. When I became tired of fighting against myself, that's when I fully felt and experienced all of those things I was trying to keep from feeling and experiencing. It was not at all easy, but this is when I realized in order to manage my emotions I first must understand them. So I took the journey of becoming more aware of who I was emotionally. (We will take this journey together in the *Be Beautiful Emotionally* book series.)

      What I eventually came to realize was that I was a woman and women have emotions. Not to say that men don't, but women experience those emotions differently. I learned first what I was, second what that meant, and third how to embrace it all. In a nutshell and to make it easy, first you're human, second it means you're not perfect, and third embracing it can simply mean accepting those facts. Eventually I came to realize there was nothing about having emotions that was wrong about me, and that I had allowed others to dictate how I should feel about myself, because I felt as though I needed to be hard like a man is taught to be. The problem was not that I had emotions. The problem was that I did not know how to control my emotions (we will talk more about controlling our emotions in the *Be Beautiful Emotionally* book series). The problem was not that I felt hurt, the problem was understanding what was going on behind the hurt. The problem was not that I felt

something, often times many things, the problem was how I managed the things that I felt.

After much work, I eventually came to a place of understanding where I no longer disliked the emotional side of me and no longer felt as though it was a weakness. As I began to learn how to manage my emotions, I began to feel confident in the fact that I had real and valid feelings and emotions, and it made me take pride in being a woman. I began to realize that I did not have to act or feel like a man in order to survive and keep my emotions under control. Being and feeling like a woman was perfectly fine with me and as I embraced it, I fell in love with that part of me. I felt empowered because I was now beginning to understand my own emotions. I no longer felt disconnected from them and I openly welcomed them as a part of who I am, what I am, and why I am.

This week is all about taking our dislikes about ourselves and changing the way we view them. When you no longer look at the things you dislike about yourself as a weakness and began to either change or embrace them as a strength, you began to feel empowered and take a sense of pride in who, what, and why you are. I used my emotions as my example, but that logic can be applied to anything. Only you can decide how you will turn what you dislike about yourself into a strength. Will you embody it and empower it by beginning to try to view it as a strength and use it as a strength? Or will you change the things that you dislike about yourself so that they don't exist anymore? It's up to you!

## WHO TOLD YOU?

In this instance, I feel that it's not so much who told me, but what told me. What told me my emotions were a bad thing and not something to embrace and feel empowered by? I would have to answer my relationships. My relationships shaped the way I thought about myself and my emotions. My relationships with not only men, but my relationship with my parents as well. In both instances, my relationships informed me that I was not strong enough to handle the hurts and disappointments that came with relationships. My relationships informed me that I cared too much about other people and my relationships with them. My relationships informed me that if I became rock hard, then I would be able to endure anything that came my way from other people.

## RECAP:

- First, understand what you are (sometimes the answer can simply just be human)
- Second, ask yourself what does that mean? (often times the answer can simply be I'm not perfect)
- Third, ask yourself how do you embrace it? (finding a way to accept those facts)
- Fighting against yourself only drains you
- When you no longer look at things you dislike about yourself as a weakness and begin to embrace them as a strength, you began to feel empowered and take a sense of pride in who and what you are

## LET'S DO THE WORK!

Directions: Using those things you listed last week that you did not like about yourself, follow the exercise each day to identify how you can change the things you dislike about yourself into a healthy trait you appreciate about yourself. Track your daily progress in your *Be Beautiful* Journal component by going through your day, recording your actions, your emotions, your thoughts, your challenges, and how you managed the overall process

**Understanding each question:**

**1. Name three positive things you can do to change the thing you dislike to a healthy trait and your reason for choosing these things.**

Changing the way we view things can have an effect on how we deal with things. It is all about perception. In the morning, find things that you can incorporate into your day that will help you change the way you look at the thing you perceive as negative. These could include pictures, songs, poems, affirmations, etc. Next, identify why you chose this method to help you change your perception from a negative one to a healthy one.

**2. How did you incorporate one or all of these things into your day today?**
Demonstrate how you actually used the things you chose in the morning throughout the course of your day. For example, if you chose listening to soft music to help you with having a bad attitude, then you may have demonstrated this by putting some

soft music on at your desk or on your phone and putting your earphones in to calm you down.

**3. Did any of them help? If so how? If not, what do you think you should change for it to help?**
Be honest about whether or not what you chose was helpful or not in achieving your goal of beginning to change this negative perception into a positive one. Explain to yourself why you thought it helped or why you thought it did not help. Sometimes when we write things out instead of just thinking about them, we are able to see clearly the effectiveness.

**Day 1:**

*Morning*

Last week I named _____
as something I did not like about myself.

Name three positive things you can do to change your dislike to a healthy trait and your reason for choosing these things.

1. _____

   _____

   I chose this because _____

   _____

2. _____

   _____

   I chose this because _____

   _____

3. _____

   _____

I chose this because _____

_____

Using one or all three, try incorporating them into your day today to begin seeing how you can use them to help change something you dislike about yourself into something you like about yourself. Revisit the exercise this evening to track your results. Use *Be Beautiful* journal component to help monitor your behaviors.

*Evening*

How did you incorporate one or all of these things into your day today? _____

_____

Did any of them help? If so how? If not, what do you think you should change for it to help? _____

_____

_____

**Day 2:**

*Morning*

Last week I named _____
as something I did not like about myself.

Name three positive things you can do to change your dislike to a healthy trait and your reason for choosing these things.

1. _____

   _____

   I chose this because _____

   _____

2. _____

   _____

   I chose this because _____

   _____

3. _____

   _____

I chose this because _____

_____

Using one or all three, try incorporating them into your day today to begin seeing how you can use them to help change something you dislike about yourself into something you like about yourself. Revisit the exercise this evening to track your results. Use *Be Beautiful* journal component to help monitor your behaviors.

*Evening*

How did you incorporate one or all of these things into your day today? _____

_____

Did any of them help? If so how? If not, what do you think you should change for it to help? _____

_____

_____

**Day 3:**

*Morning*

Last week I named _____
as something I did not like about myself.

Name three positive things you can do to change your dislike to a healthy trait and your reason for choosing these things.

1. _____

   _____

   I chose this because _____

   _____

2. _____

   _____

   I chose this because _____

   _____

3. _____

   _____

I chose this because _____

_____

Using one or all three, try incorporating them into your day today to begin seeing how you can use them to help change something you dislike about yourself into something you like about yourself. Revisit the exercise this evening to track your results. Use *Be Beautiful* journal component to help monitor your behaviors.

*Evening*

How did you incorporate one or all of these things into your day today? _____

_____

Did any of them help? If so how? If not, what do you think you should change for it to help? _____

_____

_____

You are halfway there! Your week is halfway complete. You may be feeling like you are a bad person or you may be starting to feel a little depressed about yourself. Stay strong!! Keep

locating those areas of dislike and keep working to get to the root of why you dislike this particular thing about yourself. I have to be able to identify and evaluate these areas in order to effectively begin seeing yourself in a more positive way. So keep going, keep doing the work, and pat yourself on the back for making the effort to positively invest in yourself!! You got this!

## Day 4:

*Morning*

Last week I named _____
as something I did not like about myself.

Name three positive things you can do to change your dislike to a healthy trait and your reason for choosing these things.

1. _____

   _____

   I chose this because _____

   _____

2. _____

   _____

   I chose this because _____

   _____

3. _____

   _____

I chose this because _____

_____

Using one or all three, try incorporating them into your day today to begin seeing how you can use them to help change something you dislike about yourself into something you like about yourself. Revisit the exercise this evening to track your results. Use *Be Beautiful* journal component to help monitor your behaviors.

*Evening*

How did you incorporate one or all of these things into your day today? _____

_____

Did any of them help? If so how? If not, what do you think you should change for it to help? _____

_____

_____

## Day 5:

*Morning*

Last week I named _____
as something I did not like about myself.

Name three positive things you can do to change your dislike to a healthy trait and your reason for choosing these things.

1. _____

   _____

   I chose this because _____

   _____

2. _____

   _____

   I chose this because _____

   _____

3. _____

   _____

I chose this because _____

_____

Using one or all three, try incorporating them into your day today to begin seeing how you can use them to help change something you dislike about yourself into something you like about yourself. Revisit the exercise this evening to track your results. Use *Be Beautiful* journal component to help monitor your behaviors.

*Evening*

How did you incorporate one or all of these things into your day today? _____

_____

Did any of them help? If so how? If not, what do you think you should change for it to help? _____

_____

_____

## Day 6:

*Morning*

Last week I named _____
as something I did not like about myself.

Name three positive things you can do to change your dislike to a healthy trait and your reason for choosing these things.

1. _____

   _____

   I chose this because _____

   _____

2. _____

   _____

   I chose this because _____

   _____

3. _____

   _____

I chose this because _____

_____

Using one or all three, try incorporating them into your day today to begin seeing how you can use them to help change something you dislike about yourself into something you like about yourself. Revisit the exercise this evening to track your results. Use *Be Beautiful* journal component to help monitor your behaviors.

*Evening*

How did you incorporate one or all of these things into your day today? _____

_____

Did any of them help? If so how? If not, what do you think you should change for it to help? _____

_____

_____

## CONSECRATION

This week you have worked to change your negative thoughts about yourself into positive thoughts about yourself. This is sacred work as you continue to look within yourself to make positive changes. To consecrate this work, affirm yourself and your thoughts by looking in the mirror and telling yourself you are awesome and worthy of the investment you are making in yourself. Then tell yourself you are *Beautiful*!

~~~~~

Congratulations!! You have successfully completed Week 2 of your own *Be Beautiful* Challenge: Changing the Way I Think About Myself. Take the next day off to mentally and emotionally relax, and prepare yourself for Week 3. Great job!! Go take a look in the mirror. I see the beauty shining through!

## WEEK THREE

### Naming Those Things I Am Good At Doing

*"the first step to being loved is learning to love what you see when you look in the mirror"*

— Tadahiko Nagao

When I was in undergraduate school I had absolutely no idea what I wanted to major in and what I wanted to do with my life. I went into school wanting to be a nurse, but along the way I changed my major at least three to four times. I found myself majoring in physical therapy, then I changed to education, then I changed to business management, and I eventually settled on hotel and restaurant management. There are probably a number of reasons why I went through so many majors trying to figure out which one to actually settle on, but two reasons seem to make the most sense to me. The first reason is that I had a lot of interests in a lot of different areas. The second reason was that I felt in all of those different areas there was something I was good at doing, so it was hard for me to make a decision on just one thing.

Eventually I settled on hotel and restaurant management, primarily because I loved to cook, and this allowed me to get my feet wet in the culinary world. That interest and passion has taken me through so many experiences both personally and professionally. And for anyone who truly knows me, they know I love to cook and I'm always coming with food (laugh). It is truly a passion of mine and it is one that I am very very good at doing. (We will talk more about learning and experiencing passions and interests in the *Be Beautiful* Personally book series)

As I realized my gifts and talents with cooking, I realized how it makes me feel about myself. Knowing that I am really good at something gives me confidence and makes me feel really

good about myself. I am able to take pride in the dishes and desserts that I make. When people compliment how good my food tastes, and I see a smile on their face or they close their eyes to enjoy the taste a little more intimately, I am able to say to myself "I did that". And it gives me a sense of accomplishment.

Accomplishments are a good way to keep you thinking positive about yourself. Even if no one validates your accomplishment with an expression or with their words, you have to take responsibility for finding your own pride in recognizing what you are good at doing. This is how you build confidence in yourself. This is how you begin to think positively about yourself and see yourself in a more positive way.

Now, keeping it all the way real, everything you are good at doing does not mean that it is healthy and produces healthy results. We can ask the same question we asked ourselves two weeks ago when determining our healthiness, "How does this make me a better person?" You can even take it a step further and be completely honest with yourself and ask, "Am I proud of being good at this?" and "Does being good at this bring me honor as a woman?" I will give you an example. Some of us are really good liars. We could lie ourselves out of any situation. We lie so good, we begin to believe our own lie even when we know it is every bit of a lie. But in the end, how does that make you feel about yourself as a person, and how does that bring you honor as a woman?

One thing I want you to take note of is that doing and being are two different things. I will give you an example. I can say "I am good at being a mother." That is not expressing what you are good at doing. That is expressing what you are good at being. Doing are the actions you take to be. What are the things that you **_do_** that make you a good mother? Possibly listening, giving good advice, patient? Then those are the things you are good at doing: listening, giving good advice, and being patient. Whenever you have to insert being before the description, you are not talking about what you are good at doing, you are talking about what you are good at being. Doing is an action. Being is a state of existence.

This week we are going to focus on those things we are good at doing. These are things such as cooking, singing, reading, writing, dancing, doing hair….and so on. It is important to identify those things we don't like about ourselves so that we can make the changes we need to begin feeling good about ourselves, as we have previously done. Well, it is equally important to recognize those things that we are good at doing because they empower our confidence and self-esteem, and keep us feeling good about who we are.

When I have done this exercise previously with ladies, at some point they get stuck and cannot think of anything. That is perfectly ok, do not get discouraged. This is when you press a little deeper and take a closer look at everything you do. When you press past this point, that is when you begin to find the hidden treasures within yourself and that is when you really

begin to change the way you think about yourself! I am so excited for you!!

## WHO TOLD YOU?

Earlier I used the example of being good at cooking. I have had many people compliment my food. When I first started cooking, my friends and family who found themselves digging in with a fork always responded with a compliment. These were people who I trusted and would give me honest feedback and critiques. This started building my confidence in my abilities to produce a rather tasty dish. This was healthy feedback and healthy confidence building. So I kept cooking, being brave enough to try new dishes, and sharing them with the people I trusted until my confidence in my own skills became something I no longer needed others to validate for me.

## RECAP:

- Accomplishments are a good way to keep you thinking positive about yourself
- Knowing that you are really good at something will give you confidence and make you feel really good about yourself
- You have to take responsibility for finding your own pride in recognizing what you are good at doing. This is how you begin to think positively about yourself and see yourself in a more positive way

- Everything you are good at doing does not mean that it is healthy and produces healthy results
- Doing and being are two different things
- When you press past the point of frustration from not knowing, that is when you begin to find the hidden treasures within yourself
- Remember, everyone is good at something, and even multiple things

## LET'S DO THE WORK

Directions: Each day find one thing you are good at doing. Answer the questions accordingly. If you get stuck, and cannot think of anything, press a little deeper and pay very close attention to yourself throughout the day. Don't be afraid to ask yourself questions. What did you accomplish? What did someone give you positive feedback on? What came easy to you? Track your progress, your thoughts, your feelings, and your behaviors in the *Be Beautiful* journal component.

### Understanding the Questions

### 1. I am good at...

Simply state something that you find you are good at doing. This question is important because as we work to create positive thoughts and images of ourselves, recognizing those positive things that are already in place is very helpful.

## 2. Is being good at this healthy or unhealthy and why?
Identifying whether or not this behavior is healthy or unhealthy is important. Everything we are good at is not always healthy. If someone is good at habitually lying, well that's just not healthy. The objective is to have healthy behavior as a demonstration of self-love and a healthy self-image.

## 3. If this is healthy, I can appreciate being good at this because...
Identify some reasons why you can appreciate being good at this. Ask yourself questions to make this determination. Some questions can include: Does it benefit other people in a healthy way and why? Does it benefit me in a healthy way and how? What about this makes me a better person?

## 4. Using the Feelings Inventory Wheel in the Appendix, knowing that I am good at this makes me feel...
How does it make you feel (Use Feelings Inventory Wheel in the Appendix) when you are finished or when you receive feedback?

## Day 1

I am good at _____

_____


Is being good at this healthy or unhealthy and why? _____

_____

_____

_____


If this is healthy, I can appreciate being good at this because____

_____

_____

_____


Knowing that I am good at this makes me feel _____

_____

_____

_____

## Day 2

I am good at _____

_____


Is being good at this healthy or unhealthy and why? _____

_____

_____

_____


If this is healthy, I can appreciate being good at this because____

_____

_____

_____


Knowing that I am good at this makes me feel _____

_____

_____

_____

## Day 3

I am good at _____
_____


Is being good at this healthy or unhealthy and why? _____
_____
_____
_____


If this is healthy, I can appreciate being good at this because____
_____
_____
_____


Knowing that I am good at this makes me feel _____
_____
_____
_____

## Day 4

I am good at _____
_____


Is being good at this healthy or unhealthy and why? _____
_____
_____
_____


If this is healthy, I can appreciate being good at this because____
_____
_____
_____


Knowing that I am good at this makes me feel _____
_____
_____
_____

## Day 5

I am good at _____
_____


Is being good at this healthy or unhealthy and why? _____
_____
_____
_____


If this is healthy, I can appreciate being good at this because____
_____
_____
_____


Knowing that I am good at this makes me feel _____
_____
_____
_____

## Day 6

I am good at _____
_____


Is being good at this healthy or unhealthy and why? _____
_____
_____
_____


If this is healthy, I can appreciate being good at this because____
_____
_____
_____


Knowing that I am good at this makes me feel _____
_____
_____
_____

## Day 7

I am good at _____
_____


Is being good at this healthy or unhealthy and why? _____
_____
_____
_____


If this is healthy, I can appreciate being good at this because____
_____
_____
_____


Knowing that I am good at this makes me feel _____
_____
_____
_____

## CONSECRATION

This week we worked on identifying those things we are good at doing. This is sacred work because you are paying attention to yourself long enough to recognize what you are good at doing, ultimately depositing good and positive energy back into yourself. Positivity is always a good way to build yourself up to being mentally strong and changing the way you think about yourself!! Great job!!

Consecrate your work by intentionally making time today do something for yourself that you are good at doing. Be sure to create time and space in your day to accomplish one thing you are good in. This will help you to continue to see yourself in a positive way.

~~~~~~

Congratulations!! You have made it through your third week of thinking positively about yourself!! You are well on your way to having healthy thoughts about who you are and seeing yourself for the awesome woman that you are! Just one more week to go!! You have done great so far and should be very proud of yourself! Keep up the good work!!

# WEEK FOUR

## Visualizing And Manifesting The Person I Want To Be

*"don't set sail using someone else's start"*

— african proverb

      This story is kind of funny. I have always wanted a flat stomach. I used to have one all through high school (that good ole "what I used to be in high school") because of being an athlete. But once I stopped being active in sports after high school I noticed my flat stomach turning not so flat (we will talk more about being healthy and comfortable physically in the *Be Beautiful Physically* book series). For years, I tried going to the gym to work out and get my flat stomach back, but as many of us have experienced, I started to become lazy and the gym eventually became a figment of my imagination (laughing).

      Years passed by and I never quite made it to the gym consistently enough to get my flat stomach back. But I always seem to find motivation when I saw Beyonce or Ciara on T.V. showing off their abs. Sadly enough, when I found the motivation it was always during a time that the gym was not open or was not a good time for me to go.

      After so many times of realizing the burst of motivation I received when I saw what I wanted for myself, I decided to post pictures of flat abs on my wall in my room, and I called my wall *The Motivation Wall*. It actually worked! When I rolled over and had the desire on the inside to go to the gym but just not the will to actually get up and go, I saw the abs on the wall and I immediately got a burst of motivation. I took advantage of it, put on my clothes, and either went to the gym or went somewhere to work out. Eventually I got on a schedule and joined the gym at my job. Monday through Friday, I would make it to the gym by 5:30am, work out for an hour, and head to my

desk. It became a part of my daily routine and I even began to notice a change in my health and energy.

Once I saw how motivated the abs on the wall got me and kept me, I then started adding more things to the wall to keep me motivated and encouraged. I added other pictures of the things I wanted for myself, and I added words of the type of woman I wanted to describe me as. I thought about women that I admired and I typed up the qualities in them that I wanted to bring out of myself. I typed words that I felt were thing I needed to work on for myself in order to be the whole and complete woman I wanted to be. I typed passages from the Bible that would help me stay focused on what I was trying to achieve, one in particular being Proverbs 31. And I even found quotes that spoke to the woman I wanted to be and typed them up as well.

Once I had all of these words, passages, phrases, and quotes typed up on the computer, I printed them all out in a font and color that was going to be appealing to me and make me want to look at my wall each day. I posted all of these things on my wall, and each day I either chose one word, one phrase, one quote, or one Bible verse to focus my day around. If my word was Bold, then I practiced ways in which I could be Bold throughout my day. If my word was Trusting, then I incorporated being more Trusting of others and myself throughout my day. If my word was Loving, then I practiced being more Loving in my actions and the things that I spoke throughout my day. I did the same thing with my quotes and my Bible verses.

I did not see it right away, but eventually I started noticing a difference in the way that I thought about myself and a difference in me. I noticed a difference in the way that I talked, the way that I acted, and the things that I allowed and did not allow for myself, all beginning with what I fed my mind about who I was, what I was, and what I wanted to be. Over time, all of the things that I said I wanted to be I actually became.

For our last and final week, we are going to create a Motivation Wall and practice using it every day. Your wall is going to consist of all of the positive images you choose for yourself. It is important to have and keep positive reminders around you because during the hustle and bustle of everyday life, it is very easy to forget our progress and what we still have yet to accomplish. Use your *Be Beautiful* journal component to track your progress.

## WHO TOLD YOU?

I would have to say I finally arrived at a place where I was telling myself the healthy things that I wanted to be and I intentionally went after becoming them. I looked to people who I realized had healthy traits about them and I said to myself "That is the health I want." After paying attention to myself, I started giving more care and nurturing to the good thinks I recognized about myself. I started to become the healthy version of who I wanted to be, what I wanted to be, and why I wanted to be it. I told myself!

## RECAP:

- Staying self-motivated will help you stay on track to reaching your goals
- Pictures, words, phrases and quotes, spiritual verses, and/or poems are all ways that can help you stay motivate daily
- Have an idea of the person you want to be and become
- Find things that motivate you to start seeing yourself as and becoming the person you want to be
- Nothing happens overnight. Everything is a process. Be patient with the process and let it do what it is supposed to do.

## LET'S DO THE WORK

**Directions:** Follow the directions for each day to create and use your Motivation Wall. You will use words, pictures, phrases and quotes, spiritual verses, and anything else that helps represent a positive image of yourself. This is meant to be fun! So make sure you have fun! Especially since you have done such a great job with putting much work and effort into yourself over the past three weeks!

## Day 1

Today you will create your motivation wall. For each category follow the directions to begin putting together all of the components for your wall.

Think of words that describe the characteristics that are important for you to have for yourself. For example: loving, bold, trusting, caring, self-confident....etc. Find a minimum of 16 words, but a maximum of how ever many you can think of.

| | |
|---|---|
| _____ | _____ |
| _____ | _____ |
| _____ | _____ |
| _____ | _____ |
| _____ | _____ |
| _____ | _____ |
| _____ | _____ |
| _____ | _____ |

Using the computer, books, or some you may already know, find four quotes that motivate you. If it helps, choose a particular theme for each quote. For example: a quote about following your dreams, a quote about loving yourself....etc.

Quote 1: _____

Quote 2: _____

Quote 3: _____

Quote 4: _____

Find four spiritual inspirations, something that speaks to your inner spirit. For instance, you can use a Bible verse or passage, a passage out of the book of our traditional religious belief, a spiritual quote off of the computer….etc.

Spiritual Inspiration 1: _____

Spiritual Inspiration 2: _____

Spiritual Inspiration 3: _____

Spiritual Inspiration 4: _____

Create 7 affirmations by filling in each blank space. Affirmations are things that you want to remind yourself about yourself to keep you with healthy thoughts about who you are and what you are. Example: I Am Beautiful, I Am Worth It, I Am Valuable

I AM _____

I AM _____

I AM _____

I AM _____

I AM _____

I AM _____

I AM _____

Great! You should have enough now to start your Motivation Wall. Now that you have gathered all that you want to add to your wall, you can complete this next step either on the computer or using blank paper and markers.

1. If you are using a computer, transfer all of your words, quotes, inspirational verses or quotes, and affirmations into Word. Use one sheet of paper for each word, quote, inspirational verse or quote, and affirmation. In Word, under the Page Layout Tab, make sure the Orientation of the paper is Landscape (sideways) instead of Portrait (straight up). Choose a font that is appealing to you, choose a color or colors that you like best, and choose a

font size so that is big enough for each motivation to have its own page.

EXAMPLE:

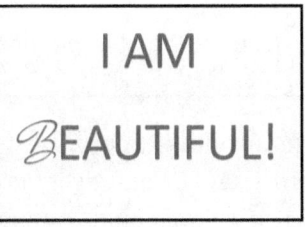

If you are not using a computer, use blank sheets of paper and markers and or colored pencils to complete the same directions above.

2. Once you have transferred all of your words, quotes, and affirmations to separate sheets of paper, find a wall in a part of your home that you frequent the most. I would suggest your bedroom because that is where you wake up in the morning and go to sleep at night.

3. Use clear tape to tape everything to your wall.

Your wall is complete!!

## Day 2

*Morning:*

Pick one word, quote, spiritual inspiration, or affirmation off your wall _____

Focus on this throughout the day. Use it to remind yourself. Use it as a reflection. Use it by putting it into practice. However you choose to focus on it throughout the day, make it the focal point of your day. Use your *Be Beautiful* journal component to track your progress.

*Evening:*

Record your experience using your word, quote, inspirational quote, or affirmation today

Did you have to use it as a reminder today? If so, how? _____

_____

_____


Did you have to use it as a source of inspiration? If so, how?

_____

_____

_____

Did you reflect on it? If so, what was your reflection? _____

_____

_____

How did it help you think positive throughout the day? _____

_____

_____

## Day 3

*Morning:*

Pick one word, quote, spiritual inspiration, or affirmation off your wall _____

Focus on this throughout the day. Use it to remind yourself. Use it as a reflection. Use it by putting it into practice. However you choose to focus on it throughout the day, make it the focal point of your day. Use your *Be Beautiful* journal component to track your progress.

*Evening:*

Record your experience using your word, quote, inspirational quote, or affirmation today

Did you have to use it as a reminder today? If so, how? _____

_____

_____


Did you have to use it as a source of inspiration? If so, how?

_____

_____

_____

Did you reflect on it? If so, what was your reflection? _____

_____

_____

How did it help you think positive throughout the day? _____

_____

_____

## Day 4

*Morning:*

Pick one word, quote, spiritual inspiration, or affirmation off your wall _____

Focus on this throughout the day. Use it to remind yourself. Use it as a reflection. Use it by putting it into practice. However you choose to focus on it throughout the day, make it the focal point of your day. Use your *Be Beautiful* journal component to track your progress.

*Evening:*

Record your experience using your word, quote, inspirational quote, or affirmation today

Did you have to use it as a reminder today? If so, how? _____

_____

_____


Did you have to use it as a source of inspiration? If so, how?

_____

_____

_____

Did you reflect on it? If so, what was your reflection? _____

_____

_____


How did it help you think positive throughout the day? _____

_____

_____

## Day 5

*Morning:*

Pick one word, quote, spiritual inspiration, or affirmation off your wall _____

Focus on this throughout the day. Use it to remind yourself. Use it as a reflection. Use it by putting it into practice. However you choose to focus on it throughout the day, make it the focal point of your day. Use your *Be Beautiful* journal component to track your progress.

*Evening:*

Record your experience using your word, quote, inspirational quote, or affirmation today

Did you have to use it as a reminder today? If so, how? _____

_____

_____

Did you have to use it as a source of inspiration? If so, how?

_____

_____

_____

Did you reflect on it? If so, what was your reflection? _____
_____
_____

How did it help you think positive throughout the day? _____
_____
_____

### Day 6

*Morning:*

Pick one word, quote, spiritual inspiration, or affirmation off your wall _____

Focus on this throughout the day. Use it to remind yourself. Use it as a reflection. Use it by putting it into practice. However you choose to focus on it throughout the day, make it the focal point of your day. Use your *Be Beautiful* journal component to track your progress.

*Evening:*

Record your experience using your word, quote, inspirational quote, or affirmation today

Did you have to use it as a reminder today? If so, how? _____

_____

_____


Did you have to use it as a source of inspiration? If so, how?

_____

_____

_____

Did you reflect on it? If so, what was your reflection? _____
_____
_____

How did it help you think positive throughout the day? _____
_____
_____

## Day 7

*Morning:*

Pick one word, quote, spiritual inspiration, or affirmation off your wall _____

Focus on this throughout the day. Use it to remind yourself. Use it as a reflection. Use it by putting it into practice. However you choose to focus on it throughout the day, make it the focal point of your day. Use your *Be Beautiful* journal component to track your progress.

*Evening:*

Record your experience using your word, quote, inspirational quote, or affirmation today

Did you have to use it as a reminder today? If so, how? _____

_____

_____


Did you have to use it as a source of inspiration? If so, how?

_____

_____

_____

Did you reflect on it? If so, what was your reflection? _____
_____
_____


How did it help you think positive throughout the day? _____
_____
_____


## CONSECRATION

This week you worked to visualize the person you want to be so you can manifest within yourself the person you want to be. This is work is sacred because you are honoring yourself in a positive and healthy way.

Consecrate this week's work by rewarding yourself. Buy yourself some pretty flowers, take yourself out to eat, make yourself your favorite dish, or anything that brings you excitement and happiness in a healthy way. You deserve it for staying and being committed!!

CONGRATULATIONS!! You have completed thirty days of developing a positive self-image! You should be so proud of yourself for sticking to it and for doing the work! No one should feel more proud than you! It took a lot of discipline and hard work creating positive thoughts about yourself over the last thirty days, but that just makes it even more of a reward!

The tools you have learned over the last thirty days will be tools that you can use throughout every phase and course of your life. It is something that has to be worked on and challenged daily, but as time goes by and you keep sticking to it, it should become easier and easier to practice.

I want to hear of your success. Please visit our website at www.iwillbebeautiful.com and leave your success story in our Success Story Bag. You can also visit our Facebook page, I Will Be Beautiful, and leave a comment on our wall of your journey and your success as a way to encourage other women to Be Beautiful just as you have chosen to do.

If you enjoyed this book and this thirty day journey, please check out all of our other Be Beautiful books at www.iwillbebeautiful.com.

Be Beautiful! Stay Beautiful!

*Keedra*

# APPENDIX

# Feelings Inventory Wheel

# *ENDNOTES*

[1] Porter, Michael. *The Conspiracy to Destroy Black Women*. Sauk Village: African American Images, 2001.

[2] Hill, Gwendolyn, Markeva. *Womanism Against Socially-Constructed Matriarchal Images: A Theoretical Model Toward a Therapeutic Goal*. New York: Palgrave Macmillan, 2012.

[3] Porter, Michael. *The Conspiracy to Destroy Black Women*. Sauk Village: African American Images, 2001.

[4] Akbar, Na'im. *Breaking the Psychological Chains of Slavery*. Tallahassee: Mind Productions and Associates, Inc., 2002.

[5] IBID

www.ingramcontent.com/pod-product-compliance
Lightning Source LLC
Chambersburg PA
CBHW020939180426
43194CB00038B/543